MINDFUL GAMES
FOR KIDS

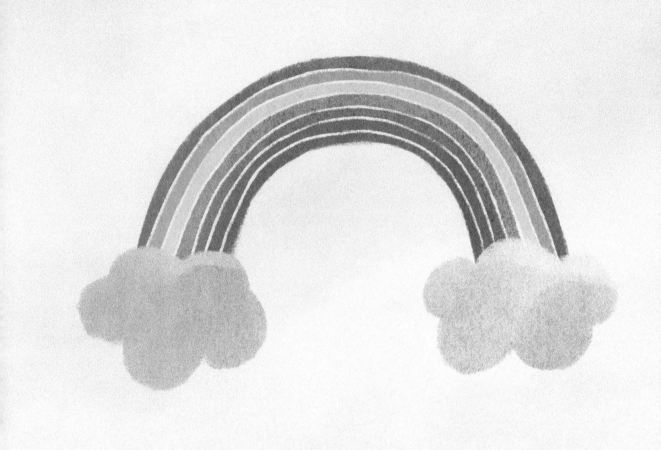

Mindful Games
FOR KIDS

50 Fun Activities to Stay Present, Improve Concentration, and Understand Emotions

KRISTINA MARCELLI-SARGENT

Illustrations by Kelsey Buzzell

ROCKRIDGE
PRESS

Interior and Cover Designer: Julie Gueraseva
Art Producer: Samantha Ulban
Editor: Lia Ottaviano
Production Editor: Melissa Edeburn
Illustrations © 2020 Kelsey Buzzell

ISBN: Print 978-1-64611-593-8 | eBook 978-1-64611-594-5
R0

To children everywhere—I hope you can use your superpower of focusing on the now to enjoy life and help others, and use your strengths and talents to make the world a better place!

Contents

Letter to Grown-Ups

Dear Grown-Ups,

You have probably heard the term *mindfulness*. Mindfulness is the ability to practice maintaining awareness in the present moment by nonjudgmentally noticing thoughts, feelings, and bodily sensations; it is paying attention on purpose (Kabat-Zinn, 2003). Research has proven mindfulness to be very helpful for adults, but not everyone understands that children also greatly benefit from practicing it. Awareness is the foundation for all life experiences and skills. When children increase their awareness in the present moment, they can increase their attentiveness, better regulate their emotions, make safer choices, and raise their awareness of others' emotions (Baer, Smith, and Allen, 2004; Diamond and Lee, 2011; Fernando, 2013). By using mindfulness to notice their own and others' emotions, children can better employ appropriate interpersonal skills (Schonert-Reichl et al., 2015).

    This book will teach children 50 fun games to begin practicing mindfulness. The games are divided into five chapters: Magic Breath (teaching children breathing techniques), Spectacular Senses (helping children connect to their five senses in the present moment), Gentle Thoughts (teaching children how to notice and manage thoughts), Easy Emotions (helping children understand and notice emotions), and My Amazing Body (helping children connect to their bodies to be more present). You can start at the beginning of the book and work your way through or jump in anywhere. Grown-ups can join in the fun, too. Feel free to read along and engage in these mindful games because, after all, mindfulness is great for everyone!

CHAPTER ONE

Magic Breath

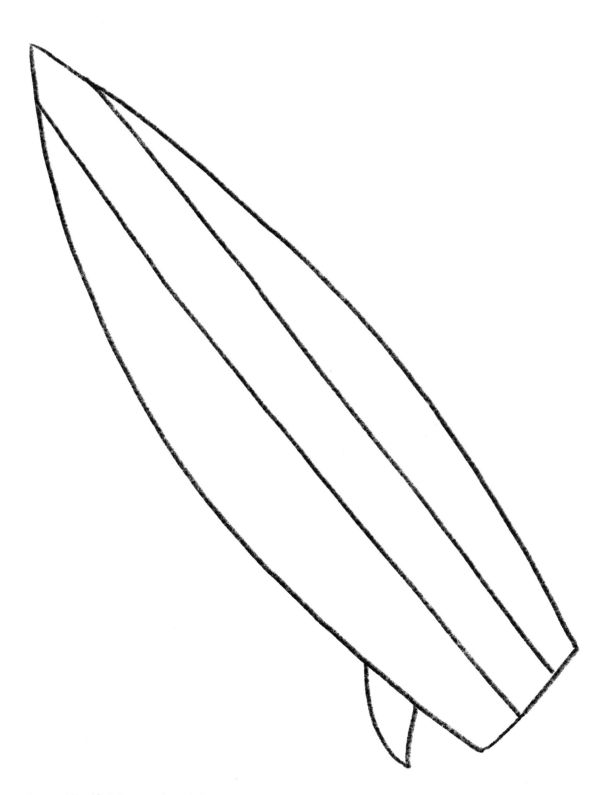

Stone Surfing

Did you know that breathing deeply into our bellies sends a special message to our brains to help us feel calm and focused? We can take deep belly breaths any time we need to feel calmer and more in control. This game helps you learn how to control your breathing and take deep belly breaths.

This game can be played alone or with others. It takes 5 to 10 minutes.

<u>Supplies:</u> Paper, a pencil, markers, scissors, and a small rock or any other small toy or object.

1. Draw a surfboard on a piece of paper or trace the picture on the facing page. Decorate the surfboard with markers if you want to.

2. Use scissors to cut out the surfboard.

3. Lie flat on your back and carefully place the surfboard on your belly. Then put a small rock or toy on top of the surfboard.

4. Now concentrate on your breathing. Take deeper breaths to make bigger waves for surfing. But stay focused! The winner makes the biggest waves without letting the rock fall off the board. If you are playing by yourself, see how big you can make your breathing waves without letting the rock fall.

5. Keep practicing! The more we practice belly breathing, the easier it gets and the more we can use it at school, home, or anywhere.

In My Heart

This breathing game helps you feel connected to people who are important to you. When we feel the love of others, we feel safe. When we feel safe, we can make safer choices, increase our willingness to try new things, and make new friends.

This game can be played alone or with others. It takes 3 to 5 minutes.

<u>Supplies</u>: A pillow or a soft place to sit.

1. Sit in a soft, comfortable spot. Try to find a place that is quiet.

2. Make your hands into a heart shape by connecting your thumbs and pointer fingers, just like the picture on the facing page. Hold your shaped hands up to your chest above your heart.

3. Close your eyes and imagine someone who cares about you, like a teacher, a parent, a foster parent, an aunt or uncle, a grandparent, a friend, or anyone who helps you feel special and safe.

4. Take deep, slow breaths while thinking of being with this person.

5. With your hands near your heart, see if you can feel your heart beat while you are breathing. Feeling it can be tricky, and it takes extra focusing powers!

6. Keep breathing and thinking of this special person until you feel completely relaxed.

7. Remember, you can carry anyone in your heart wherever you go, even when you aren't with that person or can't see them anymore. It feels good to feel safe and loved!

Mindful Games for Kids

GAME 3

Spider-Keeper Breathing

This game helps you practice noticing your body and your breathing at the same time, which can help you feel calmer.

This game can be played alone or with others. It takes 5 or more minutes.

<u>Supplies</u>: Paper and a pencil or marker.

1. Draw a spiderweb and a spider. If you'd like, you can trace the one on the facing page.

2. Pretend your spider wants to move to a new place in the room. Look around and choose a safe space for your spider.

3. Now pretend you are the wind carrying the spider. The spider needs deep, slow breaths to carry it all the way to its new spot.

4. Place the spider and the web in the palm of your hand and balance them there.

5. You can walk only when you are breathing out slowly because the wind is what moves you and the spider.

6. Continue to take very deep and slow breaths while walking carefully to the spider's new home. If you move too fast or breathe too fast, the spider will blow off your hand and you will have to start over.

7. The winner is the first person to get the spider somewhere safe by focusing on walking and breathing slowly. If you are playing by your-self, see if you can carry it all the way without dropping it. Don't give up! Even if you drop your spider, the more you practice breathing and focusing on your slow body movements, the better you get at it!

Mountain Breathing

This game helps you feel strong and connected to the ground, just like a mountain. When you feel strong and connected, you are better able to handle your emotions.

This game can be played alone or with others. It takes 3 to 5 minutes.

Supplies: Your imagination.

1. Stand with your legs apart, and put your hands together, fingers pointing upward, over your head. This position helps put you in the same triangle shape as a big, strong mountain.

2. Mountains are strong even when big storms or winds come their way! Pretend a big gust of wind blows over you. The mountain air is fresh and clean.

3. Breathe that mountain wind right in through your nose and all the way down to your belly.

4. Keep your arms up but look down with your eyes and see if you can see your belly moving while you breathe.

5. Keep breathing deeply without falling. Remember, mountains are very strong!

6. The winners of this game stay balanced and keep breathing in their bellies while standing just like a mountain! If you are playing by yourself, see how many deep belly breaths you can take while standing like a mountain.

Balloon Breathing

Did you know that imagining letting things go actually calms our brains and bodies? This breathing game gives you a chance to relax from anything that is bothering you.

This game can be played alone or with others. It takes 5 or more minutes.

Supplies: Your imagination.

1. Stand straight and tall. Close your eyes if you want to.

2. Breathe in deeply through your nose and make a gentle fist with one of your hands. You should be able to see a hole between your curled fingers and your hand.

3. Breathe out into this hole and pretend you are blowing up a balloon!

4. Keep filling it up. Pretend you are blowing out whatever you want to let go of inside the balloon. Maybe you have a yucky thought, a big emotion, or a memory you want to take a break from.

5. Once you are finished blowing the balloon up completely with whatever you want to let go of, pretend to tie it closed.

6. Now let it go! Keep breathing and blowing out long, strong breaths up into the sky to help your balloon float away!

7. It feels good to take a break from things that make us feel bad, but it is also okay to think about them sometimes. If you want your balloon back, just reach up high and grab the imaginary string attached to it!

8. Everyone wins in this game. It is okay to have big thoughts, strong emotions, and heavy memories. But sometimes we want to take a break from them and relax. So it is okay to breathe and take that break.

As Cool as a Snowflake

Did you know that your brain and body are connected and talk to each other? So, when we relax our bodies, we relax our minds, too! This game helps you learn how to focus on your body and your breathing so you can calm down and handle strong emotions.

This game can be played alone or with others. It takes 3 or more minutes.

<u>Supplies</u>: Your imagination.

1. Close your eyes and imagine you are a very special snowflake floating in the cold air.

2. Breathe in through your nose while you count to four. Pretend you are breathing in cold, snowy air.

3. Breathe out through your mouth to the count of six.

4. As you breathe out, slowly start to fall to the ground like a gentle snowflake. Don't fall too fast!

5. Keep breathing and getting lower and closer to the ground. Remember, snowflakes fall softly and gently. See how quietly you can go to the ground. The slowest and quietest snowflake wins!

6. Now that you are on the ground, pretend you are melting. Relax all the muscles in your face, your body, your arms, your legs, and your fingers. Even your toes are melting! Keep melting until you are completely relaxed and calm.

Rescue the Rain Cloud

This game helps you practice deep breathing in a way that lets you see your breath moving! With this game, you feel more in control—while having fun, too!

This game can be played alone or with others. It takes 5 or more minutes.

<u>Supplies</u>: Paper or a cotton ball.

1. Rip a piece of paper in half. Now scrunch up one half to make it look like a little rain cloud. You can also use a cotton ball for the cloud.

2. Put your rain cloud somewhere in the middle of the room.

3. Pretend that your rain cloud is stuck. Oh no! It keeps raining in the same spot. The rain cloud needs your help moving to a new place to give other people, animals, and plants some water.

4. You are the wind and you get to help the cloud. Crawl over to the cloud or sit near it.

5. Put one hand on your belly and breathe in a big gust of wind. Make sure you feel your belly moving so you are getting plenty of wind to help the cloud.

6. Now breathe out slowly and strongly through your mouth. Your breath will help move the cloud to a new place to share the rain! Thank you, wind! Keep breathing and moving the cloud. Remember, not too fast, or the cloud may go too far away!

7. The winners of this game take deep belly breaths and are focused breathing out slowly to move their cloud, just like the real wind. If you are playing by yourself, see how far you can move your cloud with your deep breaths.

Rainbow Breathing

Did you know the slower we breathe out, the calmer our brains and bodies feel? This game helps you use your imagination to practice breathing out slowly.

This game can be played alone or with others. It takes 5 or more minutes.

<u>Supplies</u>: Your imagination.

1. Find a space for a rainbow that is bigger than you but smaller than the room you are in. Now pretend you have magic breath that lets you breathe out colors, and create your own rainbow!

2. Take a deep breath in through your nose. Pretend you are breathing in the color red. Now get close to the floor where the rainbow will start, and very slowly breathe out the color red. Start to stand up and keep breathing out to paint the entire rainbow shape with your breath. Breathe out slowly so you don't run out of color!

3. Now imagine breathing in the color orange through your nose. Start down low again, right under where you imagined painting the red. Breathe out slowly so you don't run out of orange. Keep breathing out slowly until you finish the orange part of the rainbow.

4. Now add yellow. If you want to keep going, you can add green, blue, indigo, purple, and any other colors you'd like. It is your rainbow!

5. The winner of this game made the biggest rainbow and focused on slow breaths out so they didn't run out of color. Great job practicing those slow breaths out! You are in control!

My Safe Color

This game helps you feel relaxed, calm, and safe by using your imagination and breathing at the same time. Our imagination is strong and can help us, just like a superpower!

This game can be played alone or with others. It takes 5 or more minutes.

<u>Supplies</u>: A pillow or a soft place to sit.

1. Find your comfy spot and cross your legs.

2. Close your eyes and imagine a color. It can be any color you want, and it can even be more than one color!

3. Imagine that every time you breathe out slowly and calmly, you are creating a safe bubble with this color.

4. Keep taking slow, deep breaths and imagine the safe bubble growing all around you. It is your own special place to feel safe.

5. As you sit in your safe bubble, see if you can imagine breathing in this special color until it fills up your entire body, from your head all the way down to your toes.

6. Keep breathing until you are completely filled up with this color on the outside and the inside.

7. Remember, you can breathe and imagine your special safe bubble anywhere you are, to help you feel calm and relaxed. It feels good to have your own special space in your imagination!

Now You Be in Charge

This game helps you be in charge of your own breathing. You have learned all about how deep breathing helps you feel calmer, more focused, and better able to make safe choices and solve problems. You are an expert on deep breathing now and can make up your own ways to breathe!

This game can be played alone or with others. It takes 5 or more minutes.

Supplies: Your imagination.

1. Remember the most important parts of taking a deep breath: breathing in to make your belly move, then breathing out slowly, trying to stay focused on your breathing.

2. Now use your imagination and make up your own way to take deep breaths! Maybe you want to breathe out fiercely, like a fire-breathing dragon, or breathe in gently, like a sniffing puppy. You get to decide!

3. If you are in a group, teach the others about your favorite way to practice taking deep breaths. Also, listen carefully to what everyone is teaching. At the end, the one who remembers the most ways to take a deep breath wins!

4. If you are playing by yourself, count how many different ways you can take deep breaths. Teach them to someone else when you can. Remember, even grown-ups feel better when they take deep breaths, so maybe you can teach a grown-up you know, too!

CHAPTER TWO

Spectacular Senses

Senses Detective

Did you know that focusing on what is happening right now using your different senses can actually calm your body and clear your mind? This game helps you pay attention to your senses to feel more focused and relaxed. You have five senses: sight, hearing, taste, touch, and smell.

This game can be played alone or with others. It takes 5 to 10 minutes.

Supplies: A toy, blanket, or any other small object, and your senses of sight, hearing, touch, and smell.

1. Whether you have chosen a special toy, blanket, or other object. you get to be a detective and investigate it!

2. Start by noticing what your object looks like. What color is it? Move it around and see if the light reflects off it.

3. Next, hold the object in your hand. Is it soft or hard? Is it cool or warm? Is it smooth or bumpy? What else do you notice about how it feels?

4. Now see if the object has a smell.

5. Does the object make any sounds? Hold it to your ear and rub a hand over it. Do you hear anything?

6. Whoever can notice the most things about their object wins the game! If you are playing by yourself, count how many different things you can notice using your senses. Try to notice more each time you play!

Octopus Feelers

This game helps you practice connecting with the world through touch to calm your body and mind.

This game can be played alone or with others. It takes 5 to 10 minutes.

<u>Supplies</u>: Your sense of touch.

1. If you are playing with more than one player, take turns being the octopus.

2. One player pretends to be an octopus under the sea. The octopus should close their eyes and imagine sitting on the ocean floor.

3. Now, using only their sense of touch, the octopus feels around with their hands and notices the ground they are sitting on. Is it soft or hard? Is it bumpy or soft? Is it cool or warm?

4. While the octopus is noticing the ground, the other players find some different objects in the room, like toys, blankets, or other items that are safe to play with.

5. The other players quietly bring one object close to the octopus.

6. With their eyes closed, the octopus reaches for the object and feels it using only their hands. What does it feel like? Take your time noticing. The more time you take to focus, the better you will be at guessing!

7. The octopus guesses what the object is! Keep playing with different objects until the octopus figures out five different items. Then it is the next player's turn to pretend to be the octopus.

8. If you are playing by yourself, set some toys or other safe objects out in front of you and mix them up. Then close your eyes and try guessing with your eyes closed!

Smells for the Security Guard

Did you know that there's a part of your brain that acts like a security guard? It is called the amygdala. Its job is to pay attention to what is around you and make sure you are okay. Sometimes the security guard gets confused and makes you have strong emotions. This game helps you practice staying calm so you can make safer choices.

This game can be played alone or with others. It takes 3 to 5 minutes.

Supplies: Your sense of smell and a grown-up.

1. Close your eyes and think of a smell that makes you feel calm and relaxed.

2. See if you can find something that has this smell. It might be a flower from outside, your favorite fruit, a special snack, or even the clean clothes you're wearing! Ask a grown-up before you choose what to smell to be sure you pick something that is safe for your body.

3. Take a breath of this favorite smell in through your nose and pay attention to what is happening in your body.

4. Keep taking deep, slow breaths without smelling the object. Notice if you can help your body stay calm and relaxed just by thinking of the smell.

5. Everyone wins this game because it helps us feel calm and make safer choices! Remember, you can imagine your calming smell wherever you are, even when you don't have the item with you!

Fun with My Favorite Color

This game helps you practice focusing on your sense of sight. When we focus on our surroundings, we can notice where we are right now, which clears our minds. When our minds are clear, we can make safer choices and solve our problems more easily.

This game can be played alone or with others. It takes 5 to 10 minutes.

<u>Supplies</u>: Your sense of sight.

1. Think of your favorite color. It can be any color in the whole world!

2. Now you get to be a "seeing detective." Look around the room or area you are in. Count how many different things you can spot that are your favorite color.

3. When you have found at least five things in that color, start looking for another color. Find at least five things in this color, and then start over again with a new color.

4. Whoever finds at least five things in each color wins! But the game isn't just about finding all the colors first. In this game, the winner focuses and calmly notices what is in the room.

My Big Bat Ears

This game helps you focus on your sense of hearing. It helps you quiet your mind and body to pay special attention to the sounds around you, which can help you feel more focused and in control.

This game can be played alone or with others. It takes 5 or more minutes.

Supplies: Your sense of hearing.

1. Pretend you are a bat, with great big ears for hearing even the smallest sounds.

2. Take a deep breath in through your nose and then out through your mouth. Notice if you can hear your breath coming in and out of your body.

3. Check in to make sure your body is relaxed. If not, take more deep breaths to calm your body so you can be a very focused bat!

4. Now stand or sit very still. Start to count how many different sounds you can hear.

5. Can you hear any people sounds? Can you hear any air moving, or wind? Can you still hear your breathing?

6. If you have enough space, slowly move to a new spot in the room, or even to a new room. Maybe you can go near a window. What sounds do you notice now?

7. Remember to walk very slowly because you are noticing how many different things you can hear.

8. Everyone who notices different things they can hear by being very focused and quiet wins this game! If you are playing by yourself, count how many different things you can notice, and try to notice more each time you play.

The Magical Ground

This game helps you feel safe and secure by connecting you with the earth. When we focus on where we are and how we are connected to the ground, it helps us better handle our big thoughts and strong emotions.

This game can be played alone or with others. It takes 3 to 5 minutes.

<u>Supplies</u>: Your sense of touch.

1. Find a special spot to sit either inside or outside.

2. Sit and cross your legs, or stretch your legs straight out in front of you. Just make sure you are comfortable.

3. Close your eyes and pretend you have magic sensors in your hands and fingers.

4. Start feeling the ground or floor around where you are sitting. Notice if it is soft or hard. Notice if it is bumpy or smooth.

5. Now pay attention to your body sitting on the floor or ground. Feel the weight of your body connecting to the earth.

6. Take a deep breath and keep counting how many things you can notice about the ground or floor you are sitting on. Notice if your body is feeling more relaxed.

7. The winner of this game is whoever notices the most things about the ground or floor where they are sitting.

Fantastic Fruit

Sometimes we do things so quickly we do not notice them, and then we don't get to enjoy them as much. This game helps you slow down and enjoy your sense of taste.

This game can be played alone or with others. It takes 3 to 5 minutes.

Supplies: A piece of fruit, your sense of taste, and a grown-up.

1. Get one of your favorite fruits, like an orange, a mango, a raisin, or any kind of fruit you have and like! Ask a grown-up for help.

2. Pick up the fruit and hold it. Notice if it feels cool or warm. Notice if it feels dry or wet.

3. Bring the fruit to your nose and smell it. Notice what it smells like, and notice what you feel in your body when you smell it.

4. Now put a piece of the fruit in your mouth. Slowly start to chew it. Not too fast! Notice what you feel in your mouth.

5. Keep slowly chewing and notice any changes in your body.

6. Notice the fruit moving down your throat when you swallow.

7. What else do you notice in your body?

8. Everyone who eats their fruit slowly while paying attention wins!

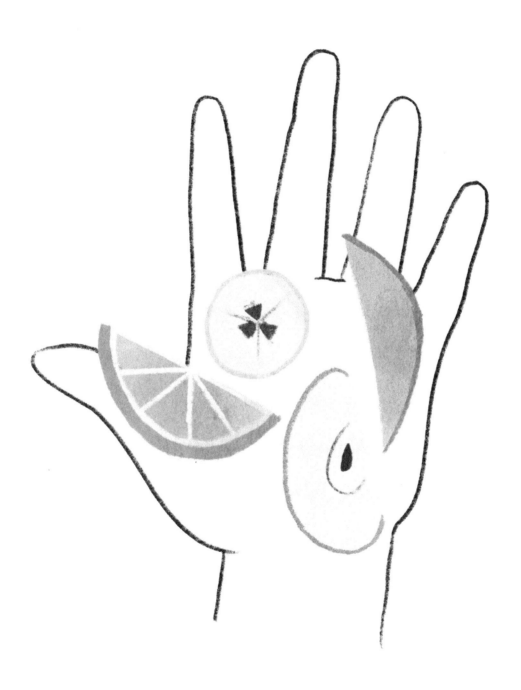

Hearing My Breath

This game helps you pay attention to your breathing using your sense of hearing, which can help you calm your body and your mind.

This game can be played alone or with others. It takes 3 to 5 minutes.

<u>Supplies</u>: Your sense of hearing and a pillow or a soft place to sit.

1. Sit in a comfortable spot. Close your eyes and start to take deep breaths.

2. Now take deep breaths in through your nose, then breathe slowly out through your mouth.

3. Use your sense of hearing to listen to your breathing.

4. Listen to the sounds of the air as it goes up, up through your nose and down, down into your body.

5. Now breathe slowly out through your mouth. Notice what the air sounds like as it goes out of your mouth and leaves your body.

6. Keep listening carefully with your eyes closed. How many different things can you notice about the sound?

7. Whoever can focus on at least five breaths using their sense of hearing wins!

Outside Adventure

This game helps you use four of your senses to focus on what is happening right now in nature! Remember, when we focus on what is happening right now, we can clear our minds and relax our bodies. The more we practice, the better we get at it!

This game can be played alone or with others. It takes 5 to 10 minutes.

Supplies: Your senses of sight, hearing, touch, and smell and a grown-up.

1. Find a safe place outside to play the game. You may need the help of a grown-up.

2. Stand still, and first notice what you see. Look around you, below you, and above you.

3. Now notice what you hear. Is there any wind? Are there sounds of people or animals?

4. Are there any leaves or rocks you can hear under your feet when you take a step forward?

5. Now press your feet into the ground. Does the ground feel soft or hard? Is it bumpy or smooth?

6. Now take a deep breath in through your nose. What do you smell?

7. Focus on your sense of touch. Can you feel any wind or sun on your skin? Is it cool or warm outside? Notice if there is anything around that you can touch, like a tree or the grass. Pay attention to what it feels like.

8. Everyone who notices the outside using their senses wins! How long can you focus?

Snake Breathing

This game helps you pay attention to your sense of hearing and your sense of touch, which helps you focus on your breathing in a special way to calm your mind and body.

This game can be played alone or with others. It takes 3 to 5 minutes.

<u>Supplies</u>: Your sense of touch and a soft place to lie down.

1. Lie on your stomach in a comfortable spot and pretend you are a resting snake, relaxing on the ground. Start to notice what the ground feels like under your body.

2. Notice if the floor is soft or hard. Notice if it is cool or warm.

3. Take a deep breath into your belly while still lying on the floor. What does it feel like? Does breathing into your belly make your back lift off the floor?

4. Now breathe out of your mouth. Stick your tongue out like a snake!

5. Notice your breath leaving your mouth over your tongue. Does your tongue feel your breath, too? Does your tongue feel cool or dry being outside your mouth?

6. Now breathe again and notice what your breath sounds like when you breathe like a snake. See if you can make a hissing sound with your tongue out!

7. All the snakes are winners in this game because taking time to relax helps us focus and make safer choices!

CHAPTER THREE

Gentle Thoughts

I Can Be a Positivity Magnet

Did you know that how we think is connected to how we feel? When we think of kind words about ourselves, we can feel happier, calmer, and less afraid to try new things. This game helps you become a positivity magnet so that positive thoughts stick to you.

This game can be played alone or with others. It takes 5 to 10 minutes.

<u>Supplies</u>: Your imagination.

1. Find a quiet spot to sit, or stand up tall and strong. Straighten your back and imagine your head lifting up to the sky.

2. Take a deep, slow breath and close your eyes.

3. Now imagine you are a magnet. But you are a special magnet, and only kind thoughts stick to you. Imagine all the happy thoughts you have about you and your life.

4. Maybe you are thinking, "I can do this!" or "I am special!" or "I am good at not giving up!" Maybe you are thinking of all the people who care about you. What other kind things can you think of?

5. Now pay attention to what is happening in your body. Are you standing straighter and taller? It feels good in our bodies when we carry kind words around with us.

6. If any yucky or unkind words pop up in your head, pretend to push them away so they don't stick to you. It can feel good to let them go. Goodbye, yucky thoughts!

7. Take another deep breath in through your nose and imagine you breathe only kind words into your body.

8. Now open your eyes and notice how you feel. Winners of this game share at least one kind thing that they thought of. Maybe it will help someone else feel good, too! If you are playing by yourself, see how many kind things you can think of and tell yourself in the mirror.

My Thinking Boat

When you notice your breathing in a focused way, you get greater control of your thoughts and emotions, which can help you feel less worried, angry, and sad. This game helps you focus on being in control of your thoughts.

This game can be played alone or with others. It takes 5 to 10 minutes.

Supplies: Your imagination.

1. Find a comfortable spot to sit or lie down, and relax your body.

2. Take a deep breath in through your nose and then breathe out through your mouth.

3. Now pretend you are on a special boat that is all yours. You are the captain, and you are in charge.

4. Here come the waves! The waves are all the things you are thinking. Some waves may be big and some waves may be small.

5. Now put your hands on your belly and take a deep breath in. Breathe out slowly. Slow breathing calms the waves in your mind.

6. If a big thinking wave comes up in your mind, just focus on your breathing again. See if you can make your breath very slow and calm to slow down the waves in your mind.

7. The more you focus on your breathing and your body by taking deep belly breaths, the more you can ride the waves in your mind. Keep breathing until the ocean feels calm and you are safe in your boat.

8. In this game, everyone wins! When we are in control of our thoughts, we are more in control of our emotions and our bodies, which helps us make safer choices and better solve our problems.

My Maze Mind

Did you know that focusing on something very calmly helps clear our minds and relax our thoughts? Some people use a special kind of calming maze called a labyrinth. This game helps you take a break from thinking to feel calmer.

This game can be played alone or with others. It takes 10 or more minutes.

Supplies: Paper and a pencil.

1. Trace the maze on the facing page.

2. Find a comfortable spot to sit with your maze.

3. Take a deep breath in through your nose and slowly breathe out through your mouth.

4. Now trace your maze with your fingertip until you complete the entire path.

5. While you are tracing the maze with your finger, keep taking deep breaths.

6. Trace your maze at least three times.

7. Now notice what is happening in your mind and in your body. Does your mind feel calmer? If not, keep tracing and focusing calmly on your maze.

8. Winners of this game have traced their maze at least three times with their finger and practiced deep breathing. If you are playing by yourself, see how many times you need to trace it to help your mind feel calmer.

start

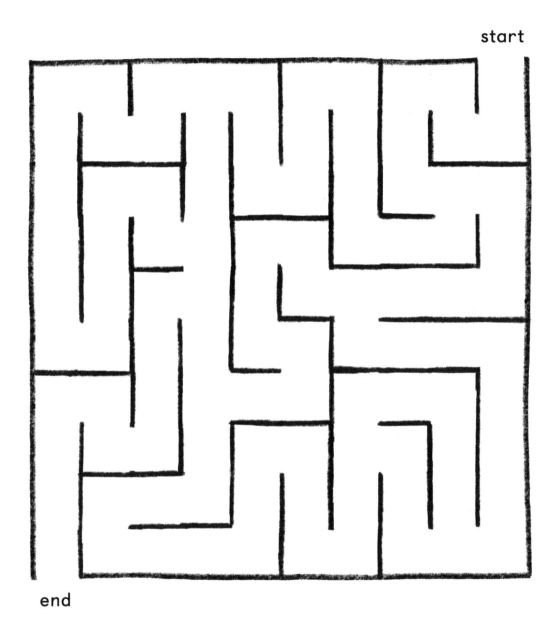

end

A Safe Place in My Hand

When we think of something scary or something that makes us mad, we end up feeling more afraid or angrier. But when we think of something that helps us feel safe, our brains and bodies really feel calmer and more relaxed. This game helps you get to that safe place.

This game can be played alone or with others. It takes 10 to 15 minutes.

<u>Supplies:</u> Paper, a pencil, and your hand.

1. Find a flat, hard place to draw and color, like a table.

2. Spread out your fingers and put your hand flat on a piece of paper.

3. Trace your hand and all around your fingers.

4. Now close your eyes, take a deep breath, and think of a time and a place where you feel the safest or happiest. Imagine everything about this place.

5. Draw or write about this place in the center of your hand drawing.

6. Now think about what you notice with your senses in your safe place. What do you smell there? What do you see there? What do you feel or touch there? What do you taste there? What do you hear there?

7. Draw a different sense in each finger of your drawing.

8. Now imagine that your safe place and all your senses are right there in your actual hand. You can carry this place with you wherever you go and think about it to help your mind and body feel safe and calm.

Magic Thought Changer

Did you know that when we notice our thoughts, we also have the power to change them? When we change our thoughts to be more helpful to us, we feel calmer, more focused, and more in control. This game helps you practice changing your thoughts.

This game can be played alone or with others. It takes 10 minutes.

<u>Supplies:</u> Paper, a pencil, and scissors.

1. Trace the magic wand on the facing page, or make and design your own! Then cut it out.

2. Find a comfortable and quiet place to sit and notice your thinking.

3. Close your eyes and start paying attention to your thoughts. What is popping up? Now decide if those thoughts are helping you.

4. If the thoughts are helping you, thank them. If the thoughts are making you feel yucky or scared, change them with your wand. Can you change the thoughts to say something nice? Can you change the scary thoughts to be funny? Can you add a helper grown-up in your thoughts so you are not alone?

5. Use your wand to pretend to change each thought to a new thought. Now notice if the new thought helps you feel better. You get to be in charge!

6. Whoever practices noticing their thoughts wins! If you are playing by yourself, see how many thoughts you can notice and how many you want to change!

Hungry Dinosaur Thinking

Did you know that the way we talk to ourselves matters? What we say in our minds can make us feel better or worse. This game helps you practice talking to yourself in kind ways.

This game can be played alone or with others. It takes 5 minutes.

Supplies: Your imagination.

1. Find a place to stand or sit up tall and strong.

2. Close your eyes and imagine you have a special pet dinosaur. It can be any kind of dinosaur you want it to be.

3. Where do you want your dinosaur to be? You decide! Find the right spot and notice what you feel in your body.

4. Imagine your dinosaur knows you are strong and powerful and able to try new things. Your dinosaur helps you be kind and brave at the same time.

5. Your dinosaur even eats your yucky thoughts. Feed your dinosaur any yucky thoughts in your head.

6. Now your dinosaur is going to tell you something special and kind that helps you be brave and feel good about yourself and other people. Maybe the dinosaur says something like, "You are special!"

7. Everyone who shares one kind thing their dinosaur told them wins! Remember, you can pretend your dinosaur is with you anywhere you are, and when you feed it yucky thoughts, it can help you practice kind self-talk! Thank you, dinosaur!

Leave Me Be

Did you know that sometimes we think so much and have so many thoughts that our brains and bodies actually get tired? We might feel grouchy, scared, or sad with all those thoughts in our head. Sometimes we just need a break! This game helps you focus on your body so you can take a break from all that thinking.

This game can be played alone or with others. It takes 5 minutes.

Supplies: Your imagination.

1. Find a place to stand or sit up tall like a big tree.

2. Imagine you have roots that go way down, deep into the ground.

3. Stretch your arms out to the sides and pretend they are your branches.

4. Now pretend all your thoughts are leaves. Shake your arms in the wind!

5. Pay attention to what your arms feel like when you shake them. If any thoughts pop up, just shake them out again and notice what you feel in your body.

6. Push your feet into the ground. Remember, you are a strong tree. Pay attention to what is happening in your feet and your legs. If it is hard to notice them, you can stomp!

7. Keep shaking your leaves and pushing your feet. Now take a deep breath in through your nose and out through your mouth.

8. Relax your muscles. What do you notice in your body now? Did these movements give you a break from your thinking? Who can focus on being a tree the longest? The more you practice, the longer you can focus and the longer you can take breaks from thinking too much. Your body and brain will appreciate the rest!

Thinking X-Ray Machine

The more we practice noticing our thoughts, the better we become at catching the thoughts that are not helping us. This game helps you practice noticing and changing your thoughts.

This game can be played alone or with others. It takes 10 to 15 minutes.

<u>Supplies:</u> Paper, a pencil, scissors, tape, a small toy, and a grown-up.

1. Trace the shape on the facing page.

2. Now cut out the shape that you traced on your paper.

3. Fold and tape the ends together so it makes a box, which is now the X-ray machine. Leave the top flap open. You may need to ask a grown-up for help.

4. One player puts a small toy in the X-ray machine.

5. Another player gets to be the X-ray doctor, who says what the toy is thinking, for example, "I can't do this."

6. Then the first player decides how this thought makes the toy feel. For example, the toy may be feeling sad.

7. If you decide the thought is not helpful, you get to change the thought to something that makes the toy feel brave and happy.

8. If you are playing alone, see how many times you can change your thoughts. Remember, the more we practice, the better we get connecting our thoughts to our feelings. Once we notice them, we are able to change them to be more helpful to us!

My Calm Mind

Did you know that when you practice noticing your thoughts and letting them go, your thoughts start to become gentler, and you have fewer strong emotions about your thoughts? This game helps you learn how to calm your mind, which can help with school, playing sports or games, and even make friends.

This game can be played alone or with others. It takes 5 minutes.

<u>Supplies</u>: Your imagination.

1. Find a comfortable spot to sit and relax. Close your eyes.

2. Start by taking a deep breath in through your nose and then out through your mouth. Focus on your breathing.

3. Now notice any thoughts that pop up in your head. Pretend the thoughts popping up are packages.

4. Just notice the packages as they come and go, but don't open them. Right now we are practicing noticing thoughts while we take a break from thinking about them too much.

5. Whenever a new thought (package) pops up, just notice it and say goodbye to the package as it moves away. New ones will come, and that is okay. We can keep practicing.

6. Whoever can sit and notice their thoughts the longest in this activity wins. Remember, the more we practice, the better we get! If you are playing by yourself, see how long you can focus, and try to beat your time by practicing longer each time.

My Full Heart

Did you know that thinking of people who care about us and love us can actually calm our minds and bodies? This game helps you practice thinking about the important people and animals in your life to calm and relax your mind and body.

This game can be played alone or with others. It takes 10 to 15 minutes.

<u>Supplies</u>: Paper and a pencil.

1. Trace the heart on the facing page. Next, think of important people and/or animals in your life.

2. Draw these people and animals in different spots on your heart. Try to keep your thinking focused on what you are doing and all these important people and animals.

3. Now find a comfortable spot to sit or lie down. Relax and close your eyes.

4. Think of all the people and animals you drew in your heart picture. Imagine each of them filling up your actual heart.

5. Try to keep your mind focused just on these important people and animals. Notice what is happening in your body.

6. You can add more people and animals if you need to. Remember, there is room for everyone in your heart.

7. If your mind starts to think of something else, bring your focus back to the important people and animals in your heart.

8. Everyone wins, because this game helps us calm our minds and bodies and remember we are not alone and that we are connected to others who care about us.

CHAPTER FOUR

Easy Emotions

How Do I Feel?

It is important to notice our emotions and know the words for how we are feeling. All emotions are okay to feel, and we can learn how to make safe choices with them. Our feelings come and go and are always changing—we can even have more than one at the same time! This game helps you practice noticing different emotions.

This game can be played alone or with others. It takes 5 to 10 minutes.

<u>Supplies:</u> Paper, a pencil, and crayons or markers.

1. Trace the faces on the facing page.

2. Now look at the emotion on each face and think of a time when you feel that way. Maybe you are happy when you are with your friends, or sad when you lose something important to you. What other situations can you think of to match the feelings?

3. Color the faces with any color you want. You might think of which color makes you think of different feelings.

4. Look at all the emotion faces and pick one for how you are feeling right now. If you want, you can circle it, or put a rock or other object on it so you can move the rock if your emotion changes later today. Remember, you may be having more than one emotion at the same time, and that is okay!

5. Everyone who shares one emotion and a time when they feel that way wins! If you are playing this game alone, find a special spot for your emotion picture, and take time to notice your different emotions every day!

Feelings Hide-and-Seek

Did you know that noticing our emotions can help us make safer choices? When we notice our emotions, we get to be in charge of them, instead of the emotions being in charge of us. All our emotions are okay to feel, and we can learn to get along with them. This game helps you notice your emotions and get comfortable talking about them.

This game can be played with two or more people. It takes 10 minutes.

Supplies: Paper, a pencil, and scissors.

1. Draw different emotion faces on paper. Some ideas are sad, angry, happy, scared, and silly. You can even think of more to make the game more challenging!

2. Cut out each face or tear them out so they are separate.

3. One player gets to hide the faces first.

4. The other players close their eyes until all the emotions are hidden.

5. Then the other players look for them!

6. When they find an emotion, they can say out loud a time when they feel that way, like, "I feel sad when my sister won't play with me" or "I feel silly when I tell funny jokes."

7. Once all the hidden emotions are found, another player gets to hide them next or make new emotions to hide!

Jealous Bugs

Jealousy is the emotion that we feel when we want something that someone else has, or when we wish our lives were like someone else's. Jealousy does not make us feel good, and it can block our minds from being able to think kind thoughts about ourselves and others. It can also block us from being able to feel happy when good things happen to others. This game helps you notice this big emotion and feel more in control of it.

This game can be played alone or with others. It takes 3 to 5 minutes.

<u>Supplies:</u> Your imagination.

1. Find a quiet place to sit or lie down.

2. Think of a time when you felt jealous. Maybe it was when you wanted something someone else had, or when someone else was getting attention, or when someone else won a game.

3. Notice what this emotion feels like in your body.

4. Now imagine the emotion is a whole army of marching ants. Take a deep, slow breath and imagine the marching ants walking away so they aren't blocking your good feelings anymore.

5. Keep taking slow breaths and imagining that the marching ants are leaving your body and freeing you so you will be able to feel loving and kind.

6. Say out loud or in your head, "I am safe. I am okay just the way I am." You can keep practicing saying this to help the ants march away.

7. Think of something you like about yourself or something you are good at, and then notice the emotions this thought brings up and how it feels in your body.

8. Take a deep breath and give yourself a hug. Maybe you can even imagine giving a hug to the person you felt jealous of.

9. Everyone who practices this game wins because when we notice and let go of jealousy, we can feel free to be more kind to ourselves and to others.

Really Feel It!

The more we learn about our own emotions, the better we can get at noticing other people's emotions. Everyone has different emotions at different times, but we can help each other with strong emotions, too. This game helps you learn to notice how other people feel by looking at their faces and the way they are holding their bodies.

This game can be played with two or more people. It takes 10 minutes.

<u>Supplies</u>: A mirror.

1. One player thinks of a big emotion to act out. Then this person looks in the mirror and makes the emotion face. Keep practicing until it looks like the emotion.

2. Now this person shows the other players the emotion using only their face and body.

3. Then the other players guess which emotion it is.

4. The other players decide what they would say to a friend who is feeling that way. If the person looks sad, the other players may say, "You look sad. Do you want to play with me?" or "Can I draw you a picture to help you feel better?" You get to decide and try things that will help this person with their emotion.

5. Keep trying different ideas until something helps the person with their big emotion. The more we practice, the better we get at helping our friends with their emotions!

6. Now someone else gets a turn to act out an emotion. How many different emotions can you act out, guess, and help each other with? Did you learn any new ways to handle strong emotions?

Guess My Emotions

We all feel different emotions in different situations. When we eat our favorite food or go to our favorite place, we may feel happy. When something important to us gets broken or lost, we may feel sad or angry. When we hear a loud noise or go to a new place, we may feel scared. This game helps you practice thinking about your different emotions while remembering that other people have emotions, too.

This game can be played alone or with others. It takes 10 minutes.

Supplies: Paper, a pencil, scissors, tape, and a grown-up.

1. Trace the image on the facing page. Cut along the outside lines, or ask a grown-up for help.

2. Fold the paper along the inside lines, then tape the corners together to make a cube. Ask a grown-up for help if you need it.

3. One player rolls the cube first. The other players close their eyes so they don't see which emotion the cube landed on.

4. The person who rolled the cube says a time when they feel that emotion—but without saying the actual word like "I feel this way when I go to the park."

5. The other players guess which emotion it is. When someone guesses the correct emotion, the next player gets a turn to roll the cube and have everyone else guess.

6. If you are playing by yourself, keep rolling the cube and see how many different situations you can think of for each emotion.

My Safe Choices

Our emotions are not the same as our choices. Even when we are mad, it is not okay to hit people or say unkind things. This game helps you practice two steps for handling strong emotions. Step 1: Notice your emotions. Step 2: Decide a safe choice for how to handle your emotions. The more we practice how to handle our emotions through playing and pretending, the easier it is to use safe choices when we actually feel them.

This game can be played alone or with others. It takes 5 minutes.

<u>Supplies:</u> Your imagination.

1. Start with practicing feeling angry. Pretend to be angry and make an angry face. Notice where you feel this emotion in your body.

2. Think of a safe choice to make with anger. Maybe your safe choice is taking deep breaths, talking to a grown-up, or changing your thinking. Practice this safe choice. Notice your body now.

3. Now pretend you are feeling sad and make a sad face. Pay attention to where you feel this emotion in your body.

4. Think of a safe choice to make when you feel sad. Maybe your safe choice is drawing a picture, talking to a friend or grown-up, or hugging a person or toy. Practice this safe choice. Notice your body now.

5. Practice these steps again with feeling afraid, silly, and any other emotions you want to practice! If you are playing with more than one person, take turns practicing the steps with different emotions.

6. Everyone who practices step 1 and step 2 for handling strong emotions wins!

Sing My Emotions

Noticing our emotions and talking about them takes practice and can help us feel more comfortable. Remember that all our emotions are okay to feel. Everyone has them! This game helps you practice getting along with your emotions and remembering safe ways to handle them.

This game can be played alone or with others. It takes 5 to 10 minutes.

<u>Supplies</u>: Your imagination.

1. Think of an emotion you want to focus on. It can be any emotion!

2. Make up a song about your emotion. Think of when you feel that way, what helps you with your emotion, and safe choices to make with this emotion.

3. Think of a beat for your song! You can clap your hands, make noises with your mouth, drum on your desk, or stomp your feet!

4. Practice your song and all the words you are singing about your emotion.

5. Share your song with others! Maybe you can help teach other people about this emotion and ways they can handle it, too. Everyone has different emotions, and all emotions are okay to feel.

6. Everyone who makes up a song about an emotion wins! If you don't want to share with everyone, you don't have to. Your song can still help you!

Big Lion Breathing

Everyone feels afraid sometimes. Sometimes this emotion can stop us from trying new things and can make it harder to remember that it is okay to make mistakes. This game helps you practice handling fear and helps you feel calmer and more confident.

This game can be played alone or with others. It takes 3 to 5 minutes.

<u>Supplies</u>: Your imagination.

1. Think of a time when you feel scared. Maybe it is at nighttime or when you are trying to do something new, like make a new friend or play a new game. It is okay to feel afraid. Everyone feels afraid sometimes.

2. Imagine a big, strong lion with you that helps you feel like you are not alone! Decide where you want your lion to sit or stand. The lion can be next to you, behind you, or in front of you.

3. Now take a deep breath in through your nose, and breathe out through your mouth. Roar like a lion.

4. Say in your head or out loud, "I can handle this! I can try new things! I am strong!"

5. Keep breathing, and repeat those words if you need to.

6. Breathing and saying kind words to ourselves are two ways that help us get along with the emotion of fear and help us feel more relaxed and confident. You can do it! What will your lion breathing help you do?

Cool Off with Ice Cream

The more we practice making safe choices with our emotions, the better we get at handling all of our emotions, even really big ones! When we make safe choices with our emotions, we feel good and are able to be kind to ourselves and others. We can also better solve our problems and focus on what we need to do. This game helps you remember your safe choices when different emotions come up.

This game can be played alone or with others. It takes 5 to 10 minutes.

<u>Supplies:</u> Paper and a pencil.

1. Trace the ice-cream cone on the facing page.

2. Now close your eyes and take a deep breath in through your nose and out through your mouth to help you focus.

3. Think of an emotion. You can start with angry, sad, scared, silly, or happy.

4. Once you choose an emotion to start with, take another deep breath and think about what helps you with this emotion. Some ideas are to talk to a friend or grown-up, cry, color or draw, jump or move your body, take deep breaths, hug a person or toy, tell yourself something kind, or imagine your safe place. What other ideas can you think of?

5. Now draw or write the emotion and the safe choice in one ice-cream scoop.

6. Keep thinking of different emotions and different safe choices for each scoop until the whole picture is filled up with your emotions and safe ideas for how to handle them.

7. Find a special spot to hang your picture where you will see it every day. This picture will help remind you of safe ways to handle emotions.

Cloudy Skies

Everyone feels sadness sometimes. We may feel sad when we can't do something we want to do, or when we see someone else feeling sad or having a hard time. This game helps you learn to get along with your sadness and remember that strong emotions do not last forever.

This game can be played alone or with others. It takes 3 to 5 minutes.

<u>Supplies</u>: Your imagination.

1. Find a comfortable and quiet spot to sit, stand, or lie down. Think of a time when you felt sad.

2. Imagine you are the great, big, blue sky. Here come some clouds. Maybe there is a stormy rain cloud of sadness, which is okay.

3. Say hello to the clouds. Hello, different emotions!

4. Take a deep breath in through your nose, and keep watching the clouds in your imagination. Maybe new emotion clouds come. Practice saying hello to them.

5. Notice if the clouds stay there or start to move. Just practice noticing.

6. Think about what you like to do when you feel sad. Maybe you like to talk to a friend, a grown-up, or a pet. Maybe you like to cry or color. Maybe you like to get a hug from someone you care about. Our choices can help blow our big emotion clouds away like the wind.

7. When we notice our emotions, we can feel better about them. We can know that all our emotions are okay to feel and they do not last forever. They come and go like the clouds!

CHAPTER FIVE

My Amazing Body

Hello, Body!

When we notice and listen to our bodies, we are better able to make safe choices and handle strong emotions and thoughts. This game helps you notice your body and thank it for all that it does. You may notice that your muscles feel relaxed, or maybe they feel tight or tired. Maybe you notice your stomach growling or your body breathing in and out. Whatever you notice, just pay attention to it while you breathe. Don't forget to always ask a grown-up for help if you notice any pain in your body that could mean you are hurt or sick in some way.

This game can be played alone or with others. It takes 5 to 10 minutes.

<u>Supplies:</u> Your imagination.

1. Find a comfortable, quiet place to stand or sit.

2. Start by noticing your feet on the floor. Now bend down and put your hands on your feet. If you cannot reach them, bend your knees a little so it is easier. Say hello to your feet. Hello, feet! Can you feel them touching the floor?

3. When you say hello to the different parts of your body, pay attention to anything you can about what your body is telling you. Emotions and thoughts will come up, which is okay. If any yucky emotions or thoughts come up, just notice them and then bring your attention back to your body.

4. Now put your hands on your lower legs. Hello, legs! Pay attention to any feelings in your lower legs. Do they feel tired, tight, or relaxed?

5. Put your hands on your knees and then your upper legs. Hello, knees! Hello, upper legs! Notice anything you feel in your knees and upper legs.

6. Put your hands on your belly. Take a deep breath into your belly while paying attention to it. Hello, belly!

7. Now put your hands on your chest. Hello, chest! Notice your breath coming in and out of your body.

8. Do this with your neck, your face, your forehead, and then your arms, all the way down to your fingers. Everyone who focuses on this activity wins! When you notice and understand your own body, you can make calmer and safer choices.

I Can Do It!

Did you know that when we focus on our strengths and feel connected to the things we are good at, we feel happy and confident? This game helps you practice feeling good about yourself and noticing that feeling in your body, which can help you try new things and feel good about other people.

This game can be played alone or with others. It takes 3 to 5 minutes.

Supplies: Your imagination.

1. Find a comfortable, quiet spot to stand or sit up tall and strong.

2. Close your eyes and imagine something you are really good at. This is your superpower and what makes you special. Maybe you are good at being funny, helping others, or making things!

3. Think of your superpower and push your chest out. Make sure your back is straight and tall. Put your hands on your hips.

4. Take a deep breath in through your nose and imagine breathing in all the good feelings about who you are and what makes you special.

5. Pay attention to what you are feeling in your body. Does your body feel relaxed? Does it feel strong? What else are you noticing?

6. Open your eyes and try to carry this feeling with you all day! Everyone who practices closing their eyes and noticing their bodies with their superpower wins. Can you share with others what your strengths and superpowers are? How can you use your super-powers to help other people, too?

Rainbow Waterfall

When we take time to listen to our bodies, we notice what our muscles are doing. When we are feeling worried or angry, we might have tighter muscles because they are holding on to the emotions and what is bothering us. This game helps you pay attention to your body so you can unwind and relax.

This game can be played alone or with others. It takes 3 to 5 minutes.

Supplies: Your imagination.

1. Find a comfortable, quiet place to sit.

2. Take a deep breath in through your nose, pulling the air in and all the way down to your belly. Then slowly breathe out through your mouth.

3. Close your eyes and imagine a rainbow of all your favorite colors.

4. Pretend that this rainbow is a flowing waterfall and you can step underneath it.

5. Imagine all your favorite colors flowing over your head. Imagine the waterfall relaxing the muscles in your face and jaw and all the tiny muscles around your eyes.

6. Now imagine the color flowing down your neck, across your shoulders, and down your arms and fingers. The colors calm all your muscles. Notice if your muscles are feeling looser and more relaxed now.

7. Finally, imagine the waterfall pouring over your chest and belly, all the way down your legs to your toes. Pay attention to each part of your body as you imagine this.

8. Everyone wins for practicing and feeling more relaxed in their whole bodies! Can you share with others which colors are in your special waterfall?

My Strong Heart

When we take time to notice our bodies working, we can relax them. This game helps you practice calming your strong emotions.

This game can be played alone or with others. It takes 3 to 5 minutes.

<u>Supplies</u>: Your imagination.

1. Find a space where you will have room to jump or move your body in some way.

2. Start to move! Maybe you will dance, jump, run, or swing your arms! Move in whatever way feels right for your body.

3. Keep moving until you notice a change in your breathing. Once you start breathing faster, pause!

4. Close your eyes and put your hands on your heart. Can you feel your heart beating?

5. Keep paying attention to your heart. Maybe it's beating faster. Maybe it is thanking you for the exercise, because exercise and moving are good for your body, too.

6. Now start moving again but move more slowly this time. Is your breathing getting slower, too?

7. Pause again! Listen to your heart now. What are you noticing? Can you still feel it? Are you still breathing more slowly?

8. Everyone who practices paying attention to their heart beating wins. When you are completely calm and relaxed, see if you can still notice your heart beating. You may need extra focus because your heartbeat will be softer!

My Animal Friend

Did you know that when we change how we sit, stand, and move, we can actually change how we feel and think? When we stand up tall and strong, we can feel more confident and ready to try new things. This game helps you practice changing how you move and hold your body to feel more focused and safe.

This game can be played alone or with others. It takes 3 to 5 minutes.

Supplies: Your imagination.

1. Find a comfortable spot to sit or move around if you can and want to.

2. Imagine an animal that helps you feel safe and good about being you.

3. Pretend you are this animal. Sit, stand, or move like this animal. Pay attention to what is happening in your body. What do your muscles feel like when you pretend to be this animal?

4. Now pretend that even when you are back to being a person, you can still hold all the goodness of being this animal in your own body.

5. Stand, sit, and walk like a confident person now. What do you notice in your body now?

6. Whoever practices this game using their body wins! How many different animals can you pretend to be using your whole body? How do you feel after paying special attention to your body?

Bee Breathing

When we pay attention to how we breathe, we can feel more calm, relaxed, and better able to focus. This game helps you learn a new way to breathe while noticing your body at the same time.

This game can be played alone or with others. It takes 3 to 5 minutes.

<u>Supplies</u>: Your imagination.

1. Find a place where you will have room to move and stretch out. You will pretend to be a buzzing bee!

2. Start to move your arms up and down like a bee's wings.

3. Begin slowly, then start to move them faster. What are you noticing in your arms and in the rest of your body? How fast can you move your arms? How slowly can you move them?

4. Now rest them. What do you notice in your arms now? Do they feel tired? Do they feel like they have more energy?

5. Take a deep breath in through your nose. Make sure it is a deep breath and your belly moves, too.

6. Breathe out through your mouth while making a buzzing noise like a bee!

7. What do you notice in your face and throat when you make the buzzing sound?

8. Who can breathe out the slowest, making the bee noise last the longest? Remember, the slower we breathe out, the more relaxed and calm our brain and body will feel!

Snowy Me

Did you know that when we focus on relaxing our bodies, we get a nice break from our emotions and our thoughts? This game helps you focus on relaxing your body to feel calmer.

This game can be played alone or with others. It takes 5 to 10 minutes.

Supplies: Your imagination.

1. Find a comfortable, quiet place, and lie on your back. You can also sit.

2. Rest your arms by your sides and stretch out your legs.

3. Pretend you are a soft, cold pile of snow. Uh-oh, here comes the sun! Pretend the sun is going to melt you into water for the plants and trees to drink.

4. Imagine the sun is warming and melting your snowy face. Relax the muscles in your forehead, your face and your jaw and around your eyes.

5. Now relax the muscles in your neck, chest, and shoulders, all the way down to your arms and fingers. Feel your body getting heavier as it melts into the ground.

6. Let the warm, cozy sun relax your stomach, making your breathing slow and soft. Let the sun relax and melt your snowy legs, all the way down to your toes. Imagine you are melting until you are completely relaxed and calm.

7. When you are ready, slowly stand up like you are growing into a tree.

8. Stretch all the way up and reach your arms into the sky. Everyone who focuses on this game wins because it feels good to notice and relax our bodies!

My Body Filled with Kindness

When we help other people or act in kind ways, we feel happy. This game helps you really connect with your body when you are feeling good after being kind to others.

This game can be played alone or with others. It takes 10 minutes.

<u>Supplies</u>: Paper and a pencil.

1. Think of something kind you would like to do today. You could help a grown-up, hug a friend, or say something nice to someone. You could even say something nice to a special toy or do something kind for a pet.

2. Practice making the kind choice!

3. Now find a comfortable spot to sit or lie down.

4. Close your eyes and pay attention to what it feels like in your body when you think about doing something kind. Pretend you are scanning your entire body like an X-ray machine.

5. Start at the top of your head and scan down, all the way to your toes. Can you notice your breathing and your heart beating? What else can you pay attention to in your body?

6. Draw what you noticed in your body on your piece of paper. Check in with your body. Are the good feelings growing? Now do the kind thing that you thought of for real. Everyone wins in this game because being kind to others feels good!

Stretchy String

Sometimes we hold strong emotions and worries inside our bodies, which can make our bodies feel tight and uncomfortable. This game helps you stretch and relax away any yucky feelings you may be carrying in your body. You will feel more focused and in control.

This game can be played alone or with others. It takes 5 to 10 minutes.

Supplies: Your imagination.

1. Find a quiet, comfortable place where you have room to stretch out. You can sit or stand.

2. Imagine you are a stretchy string! What color string do you want to be?

3. Now reach up to the sky. How far can you stretch? Imagine you are letting go of anything that doesn't feel good in your body.

4. Keep stretching farther and farther, and imagine letting go of any yucky feelings in your body. Stretch it out!

5. Now reach down to your toes. How far can you reach? Feel the stretch in your legs. What is your body telling you now?

6. Remember that thoughts and feelings will come up. Just practice noticing the thought or feeling and then saying goodbye to it and listening to your body again.

7. What other ways can you stretch? Who can think of the most ways to stretch their whole body? If you are playing by yourself, see if you can make up new ways to stretch and teach someone you know!

My Body Talks

Our bodies are so amazing that they actually talk to us! When we listen to them, we can relax and feel more connected to them. This game will help you listen to your body and hear what it is telling you today. Remember to ask a grown-up for help if you notice any pain in your body that could mean you are hurt or sick in some way.

This game can be played alone or with others. It takes 5 to 10 minutes.

<u>Supplies:</u> Paper, a pencil, and crayons or markers.

1. Trace the image of the person on the facing page.

2. Now find a comfortable, quiet place to lie down.

3. Listen to your body. Pretend you have a scanner that looks at the outside of your body and listens to the inside.

4. Start scanning at the top of your head, and scan all the way down to your toes.

5. Are you noticing anything that feels relaxed, or anything that feels tight or tense? Anything that feels heavy or light? What feels good? What else can you notice about your body right now?

6. Draw what you noticed happening on the person you drew.

7. Whoever shares what they noticed wins! If you are playing by yourself, see how many different things you can pay attention to about your body today. If you play this game again, see what is different from the last time you played. Our bodies often have different things to tell us every day!

Where to Learn More about Mindfulness

Calm Kids: Help Children Relax with Mindful Activities **by Lorraine E. Murray, 2012.**
This book helps adults help children learn mindfulness. It includes activities and ways to integrate a mindful perspective into everyday living for all ages.

Peaceful Piggy Meditation **by Kerry Lee MacLean, 2004.**
This children's picture book helps introduce kids to mindfulness and how to practice seated stillness with engaging illustrations.

The Power of Showing Up: How Parental Presence Shapes Who Our Kids Become and How Their Brains Get Wired **by Daniel J. Siegel and Tina Payne Bryson, 2020.**
This book helps parents learn four effective brain-based ways to mindfully "show up" for their children and foster healthy development.

Ursula Unwinds Her Anger **by Kristina Marcelli-Sargent, 2014.**
This children's picture book teaches awareness of one's emotions in the moment, how to recognize the emotions of others, deep breathing, and assertiveness skills.

References

Baer, Ruth A., Gregory T. Smith, and Kristin B. Allen. "Assessment of Mindfulness by Self-Report: The Kentucky Inventory of Mindfulness Skills." *Assessment* 11, no. 3 (October 2004): 191–206.

Diamond, Adele, and Kathleen Lee. "Interventions Shown to Aid Executive Function Development in Children 4 to 12 Years Old." *Science* 333, no. 6045 (August 2011): 959–64. http://doi.org/10.1126/science.1204529.

Fernando, Randima. "Measuring the Efficacy and Sustainability of a Mindfulness-Based In-Class Intervention." Accessed November 24, 2019. https://www.mindfulschools.org/pdf/Mindful-Schools-Study-Highlights.pdf.

Kabat-Zinn, Jon. *Mindfulness Meditation for Everyday Life*. New York: Hyperion, 2003.

Schonert-Reichl, Kimberly A., Eva Oberle, Molly Stewart Lawlor, David Abbott, Kimberly Thomson, Tim F. Oberlander, and Adele Diamond. "Enhancing Cognitive and Social-Emotional Development through a Simple-to-Administer Mindfulness-Based School Program for Elementary School Children: A Randomized Controlled Trial." *Developmental Psychology* 51, no. 1 (2015):52–66. http://doi.org/10.1037/a0038454.

Acknowledgments

Many thanks to all of those whose research and teachings on mindfulness have already changed us, as human beings, for the better. I also want to personally thank the children who have reminded me, time and again, that we were created to be playful, resilient, and above all, present. Often, it is we adults who learn from children about being mindful and connecting with life in the moment. Thank you!

About the Author

Kristina Marcelli-Sargent is a licensed mental health therapist currently practicing in rural Colorado. Kristina has more than 10 years' experience working with children, families, and adults in foster care, school-based mental health programs, partial hospitalization environments, and outpatient trauma-focused treatment settings. She has authored and illustrated several children's books, including *Ursula Unwinds Her Anger* and *Buttons the Brave Blue Kitten*. Kristina lives and plays in the mountains with her husband, Adam, and two dogs, Fresca and Joey.

CPSIA information can be obtained
at www.ICGtesting.com
Printed in the USA
BVHW051421051020
590183BV00005B/6